MW00974161

THE
CHRISTMAS
DOCTOR

THE
CHRISTMAS
DOCTOR

The True Story of Dr. J. P. Weber

• • • • • • • • • • • • • • • • • •

T O M   W E B E R

authorHOUSE®

AuthorHouse™ LLC
1663 Liberty Drive
Bloomington, IN 47403
www.authorhouse.com
Phone: 1-800-839-8640

© 2013 by Tom Weber. All rights reserved.

No part of this book may be reproduced, stored in a retrieval system, or transmitted by any means without the written permission of the author.

Published by AuthorHouse   12/10/2013

ISBN: 978-1-4918-1561-8 (sc)
ISBN: 978-1-4918-1560-1 (hc)
ISBN: 978-1-4918-1559-5 (e)

Library of Congress Control Number: 2013916580

Any people depicted in stock imagery provided by Thinkstock are models, and such images are being used for illustrative purposes only.
Certain stock imagery © Thinkstock.

This book is printed on acid-free paper.

Because of the dynamic nature of the Internet, any web addresses or links contained in this book may have changed since publication and may no longer be valid. The views expressed in this work are solely those of the author and do not necessarily reflect the views of the publisher, and the publisher hereby disclaims any responsibility for them.

John Weber was born at Creston, Iowa, in 1888. At the age of eleven he realized he wanted to become a doctor.

After finishing the eighth grade in 1904, John rode the rails to Montana to help lay railroad tracks, intending to save his wages in order to continue his education. Treated brutally by his foreman, he left the railroad construction job and traveled to Portland, Oregon, searching for work in the lumber industry.

The young man from Iowa fell victim to a pickpocket on the streets of Portland. All his savings were gone. Unable to find any job, John sank into illness and despair. During the Christmas season, 1904, his life was saved by a deeply religious nurse. He promised her he would pay her back by helping others.

John financed his undergraduate education by laboring on the railroad in Iowa. Then he worked his way through medical school in Chicago by loading and unloading freight at a railroad station each evening.

Motivated by what the kind nurse at Portland had done for him, John became a courageous country doctor in the wilds of Idaho. This is his story.

This picture of Dr. Weber was taken when he graduated from medical school in 1917.

INTRODUCTION

My father, Dr. John Peter Weber, was a country doctor. He was fifty-eight years old when I was born in 1946.

I loved to play checkers with him. It was great when he came to the Little League baseball games and watched me pitch. And I admired the way he spoke warmly to each person we met as we walked down the sidewalk.

Whenever we were at a sporting event he would run out onto the field to help a player who was injured. When he saw a wreck while driving he would pull over to the side of the road, grab his bag and run over to see if he could help. I watched him struggle to open many a badly bent car door, sometimes in terrible weather.

When I was a little child there was a boy in the neighborhood who was hit by a car and badly injured.

Daddy and me

I stood in the weeds at the side of the road and watched my father bandage and splint his broken body. I will never forget the boy's cries and moans of pain as my father loaded him into the back seat of our car. The boy looked like a mummy. Fortunately, he recovered fully from his many fractures at the hospital.

I loved to go on house calls with Dad. During the winter of 1953-1954 a woman at a remote farmhouse was expecting a baby. Dad took me along one day as he went out to see how she was doing. After awhile he came out of her bedroom into the living room and invited me to come in.

She lay in bed on her back. Dad had me touch her huge tummy, which I very shyly did. I could feel the baby kicking. The mother smiled at me as I did so.

Dad took me along the day he went out to deliver her baby. The woman was yelling and screaming as I sat in the living room. I had never heard such a racket. Finally, Dad came out of the bedroom and said, "Let's go, Tommy." As we walked toward the car I said, "What happened, Daddy? Did she die?" He put his arm around my shoulder in that companionable way of his and said, "No, Tommy, it was a normal delivery. Some ladies just make a lot of noise while they're having a baby."

One day we drove to a town in the mountains called Rocky Bar to see a sick old man. As we rode along, hundreds of jackrabbits suddenly swarmed onto the dirt road ahead of us. Dad stopped the car and we sat there for about fifteen minutes laughing as we watched the rabbits pouring out of the sagebrush onto the road. Finally the way cleared and we continued on. I can remember Dad apologizing to the elderly patient for the "jackrabbit delay."

His generosity could be quite startling. He never made much effort to collect from people. If he took care of a member of a family during an illness and they didn't pay him, he would still give the family care the next time they asked for it.

Many times I saw him tell a patient he or she didn't have to pay him anything. "You need it worse than I do," he would say. One day when I was a teenager I was helping him in his office by doing some paperwork. He spent quite a bit of time with an old fellow, removing a boil from his back and advising him concerning his diet. When the patient got up and left, I gave my father a disgusted look and said, "Well, Dad, you forgot to charge the patient anything again." He laid his head back and laughed.

Dr. Weber believed that a physician should stay with the patient, even for long periods of time, if necessary. I could give many examples of this but one will suffice. I was home from college during Christmas vacation, 1968. The phone rang about midnight. Of course it was for Dad.

It was a scene I had witnessed many times, him pulling on his clothes in the middle of the night, muttering to himself, checking to make sure he had what he needed in his bag, and then throwing on his overcoat. The outside door happened to be in my bedroom and as he opened it to leave, snow and cold air poured onto my head. I got up and watched him strut out to the car with a determined look on his face.

He didn't get home until nine in the morning. Mother asked where he had been all night. He said that the call had been from the manager of a local flophouse. A derelict man living there was very sick. "Well, I got there," he said, "and I could see the old fellow wasn't going to make it through the night. I didn't want him to have to be alone when he died so I stayed there with him. When he died this morning I filled out the death certificate, called the mortuary and then came home." Dad was eighty years old at the time.

My father died in 1976, and thereafter I felt a strong desire to gather the precious experiences of his life. I began actively seeking information in 1978. I started with an ad in the newspaper in an area in which he had lived. As a result, I met many of his former patients and friends. Eventually I moved on to the other places he had lived and interviewed many of his former acquaintances.

I learned of my father delivering a baby boy, Eddie, in 1928. The family was indigent. Dr. Weber developed a special love for the little fellow.

In 1935 the child was hit by a drunk driver while crossing a street, his body thrown 150 feet into a vacant lot by the impact. When Dr. Weber got there he found Eddie's head was broken open. He lived with the family during the Christmas season, putting the boy's skull back together. Eddie lived to be an old man.

I was told of the time during the late 1920's that a man working at a mine on the South Fork of the Clearwater River was experiencing severe abdominal pain. Dr. Weber drove over a dirt road to the mine and decided it wasn't a good place to perform an appendectomy. He lifted the miner to the back seat of his car and began driving up the road on the side of the canyon, planning on performing the operation at a small town named Mount Idaho. A tremendous rainstorm ensued and the car slid to the edge of the cliff on the right side of the road. While the car teetered in the heavy rainstorm, Dr. Weber reached into the back seat of the car and removed the man's appendix. He then fashioned a crude sled using rope and tree boughs, his car bumpers serving as runners, and pulled the miner through the mud to a house at Mount Idaho where he recovered fully.

I learned of very difficult trips made in wagons and sleds pulled by horses to remote parts of Idaho County to see patients. I saw some of the old roads he had driven his car over, narrow dirt roads that rounded the dizzy edges of high precipices, frightening roads he had traversed under all weather conditions.

Then there were the horseback rides over Pittsburgh Saddle into Hell's Canyon during winter to care for people in Oregon. I learned of hikes he made at night across the frozen Snake River in Hell's Canyon, hunched against the weather, the river groaning under the ice like a dying animal. The surface was anything but even, replete with mounds and bizarre formations, haunted sculptures of rime. There was the night he got to the ferry that crossed the Snake River in Hell's Canyon and found the operator was not present. Dr. Weber knew the patient desperately needed him. He tied his bag to his back, shinnied up to the ferry cable, grasped it with hands and legs and thus worked his way to the Oregon side while the river roared beneath him.

And on and on.

I met Nancy Jacobsen, whose connection with Dr. Weber is briefly set forth in Chapter Three, on a few occasions in my youth. Dad and I would drive to Portland and visit her home there. She was a frail old woman. I watched her and my father dance together at social functions held in the Portland area for senior citizens. They danced beautifully together.

The story of Ruth Schafer is told in Chapter Five. She and her family have long been friends of Dr. Weber's family.

Muggs Bentley, who is introduced in Chapter Six, was very helpful in giving me reminiscences of my father. He and his father, Ernest, accompanied Dr. Weber on many difficult trips to see patients.

I want to express a special thanks to Eva Taylor, who homesteaded for many years with her husband, Elmer, at Horseshoe Bend on the Salmon River. She gave me many precious recollections of my father's work in the Joseph Plains area. This wonderful woman was present during some of the operations my father performed on kitchen and dining room tables, faithfully holding a lantern so he could see. I also want to thank Len and Grace Jordan for their memories of Dr. Weber's activities in Hell's Canyon.

The reader might be surprised at how well people remember a visit from the doctor after many years, even the very words which were spoken during a physical examination or while eating at the dinner table. I know I was.

This book results from a genuine search for the truth. Every effort has been made to portray events exactly as they occurred. I interviewed my father extensively prior to his death in 1976. Even the conversations and descriptions written herein were given to me by him or some other person who was present on the occasion being narrated. The names of a few of the individuals mentioned in this work have been changed to protect their identity.

When my father was old, even in his eighties, he had unbelievably powerful arms. They were like iron. I never understood why that was until I researched his life.

The reader might be interested to know that when he was on his deathbed, he tapped me on the forearm and said, "Tommy, I practiced medicine fifty-three years and I never turned down a call. Not a one."

The people I met on my sojourns to the areas where he had lived were truly "Dr. Weber's people." They, the areas, and the houses he had visited seemed very familiar to me, though I had never seen any of them before. As I look back, it seems as if my father and I and all these people, even the locations, were closely associated in some existence prior to this earth life. Somehow we have always been together.

Tom Weber

Celebrity Comments Concerning Portions of *The Christmas Doctor*

NOTE: None of the people listed below read this entire book. Each of them read some portion of it.

Hugh Carey, former Governor of New York: "Thank you for sending me the story which related to your father. It is truly worthwhile reading."

Astronaut *James McDivitt:* "[Your father] was a great man. It's too bad we don't have more people like him living today."

Writer *William Dietrich:* "Thanks for sharing your wonderful, charming story about your father. I had an opportunity to raft the Middle Fork of the Salmon a few years ago so I'm somewhat familiar with the ruggedness of the country you describe. Your father must have been a remarkable man . . . . You have a nice gift for description."

Former Senator *Charles Percy:* "I read with great interest your wonderful story about your father, Dr. J.P. Weber. I shall long remember it."

Former Senator *Barry Goldwater:* "Thank you so much for sending me that wonderful story. I really enjoyed it. You were very kind to send it to me to read, and having read it I don't think I will ever forget it."

Author *James MacGregor Burns*: "Thanks for 'Christmas Eve 1927.' You are a fine writer—keep it up!"

Writer *Studs Terkel:* "It was a lovely and deeply moving story. Your father must have been a wonderful man and a country doctor in the noblest sense of the word."

Writer *Tony Hillerman:* "I can't remember ever reading a better description of a bitter cold night than your powerful account of the good doctor's ride with Muggs. It rings with truth (and kindness)."

Fred Chappell, poet and writer: "Thank you for sending me the lovely Christmas story, so sad and yet so joyful. I have admired the experience you've recounted and enjoyed its memory."

Historian *Merle Curti:* "Thank you deeply for . . . the story of your father . . . and its reminder that something beautiful exists along with all the indifference and emptiness."

Writer *Clive Cussler:* "Thank you for . . . the touching story about your father. A pity men like him aren't around anymore. He was a giant in his time."

Writer *Loren D. Estleman:* "Thanks very much for . . . the moving story about your father. I lost my own father in February and have been remembering a good deal since and know something of your emotions in putting this fine recollection on paper. I will treasure it."

Former Supreme Court Justice *William J. Brennan:* "Thank you for sending me that wonderful piece about your father. Dr. Weber sounds like a very delightful and caring man."

Writer *Bernard Siegel:* "Bless you for sharing. I'm going to read . . . [your stories] to medical students and doctors who forget what medicine is all about."

Writer *Vince Bugliosi:* "This is going to have to be a short note, but I just wanted to tell you how much I appreciated hearing from you and receiving the brief but very moving true story you wrote . . . . You write very well. And there indeed was a message to the story. Your father sounds like a great man, and the message of the story is a timeless one of love and compassion for one's fellow man being more important than anything else in life."

Writer *Russell Baker:* "You have written a fine tribute to your father and . . . a very good story with a strong punch. It makes us remember a time when the doctor was a truly heroic figure."

Journalist *Hugh Sidey:* "Yours was a touching story of your father . . . . His kind made this country great."

Actor *Robert Mitchum:* "Tom, thank you for the inspiring story of a modern day saint."

Correspondent *Arnaud de Borchgrave:* ". . . [You are] a writer with promise."

Writer *Norman Corwin:* "Thank you for sending me . . . 'Christmas Eve 1927.' I found . . . [it] very moving, and a wonderful tribute to a quite wonderful man in your father. He brought nobility to the medical profession, and you have reason to be proud of him."

Actress *Kim Hunter:* "Thank you very much for your letter and the extraordinary story about your father, Dr. Weber. I found it very moving and inspiring and am most grateful to you for sharing it."

Writer *Bill Pronzini:* "I found the . . . [information] about your father's courageous medical career to be interesting indeed. He must have been a truly heroic figure, of the sort that, sadly, is seldom found these days . . . . Thanks for the copy of 'Christmas Eve 1927.' I did indeed enjoy it. And it is well-written—suspenseful and moving too."

Bess Myerson: "I read . . . [your story] with close attention and interest. An unusual story about an unusual man especially in these days when dedication and caring are endangered qualities of character . . . . How fortunate you are to possess (and to have been a part of) those memories of a good man adding a human touch to so many lives—and in the old definition of a decent, good neighbor, leaving his world a little better place than he found it. Hold tightly to the treasure of those memories."

Writer *Pat Booth:* "Your story is really very touching. Keep on writing. I know how hard it is!"

Writer *Erma Bombeck:* "I read your story . . . and it is beautiful . . . . As for your writing, you're good—very good."

Judy Collins, singer and writer: "This story of yours is, in fact, beautifully written, wonderfully felt and full of feeling. I want to encourage you to write more . . . . Your writing is evocative of my own love of the West . . . . [Others] would love your story, as I do!"

Former Senator *Margaret Chase Smith:* "Your thoughtful and most meaningful story is just in and I am deeply touched. It is not only well written but certainly something that should be read by everyone."

Actress *Julie Harris:* "Thank you so much for your very moving . . . [story] about your father. I am really thrilled to read about him and his heroic deeds. What a wonderful doctor. I wish I had known him."

Tipper Gore: "Thank you for sending me this beautiful story about your father and the majestic country where he lived and practiced. Your writing has that special quality that takes a reader to the time, place and mood you describe. You certainly have captured a very moving experience with great skill and gentleness."

Actress *Liv Ullmann:* "Thank you for your lovely story. You have a wonderful father to remember. I am very moved. Nothing in the world means more than what you write—that we must all learn to love our neighbors as ourselves."

Writer *Joan Didion:* "Thank you for sharing the very moving story about your father. I got out the atlas to trace his way from Whitebird to the Snake and had a very vivid sense of him there . . . . I grew up in Northern California and so had some idea of the country—but you convey it so well."

Writer *Scott Turow:* ". . . [I receive] a lot of manuscripts . . . . Most I never read beyond a sentence or two. Yours is probably the best-written and most worthwhile I've yet received."

Former Attorney General *Griffin Bell:* "I have now read . . . [your story] and did enjoy it. It was poignant and was also a reminder of what made our country the great country that it is. Dr. Weber must have been a great man and a cut off of what we all imagine as a wonderful doctor of another time. He not only made house calls, but under the most trying circumstances."

Journalist *Seymour Hersh:* "It's a marvelous story about a day and a morality that doesn't seem to exist anymore."

Writer *Pat Conroy:* "Tom—Great story."

Football coach *Johnny Majors:* "Thank you for your letter and the fantastic story about your father. I truly enjoyed the story and I am anxious to read it to my young grandson. It is a beautiful Christmas story."

Writer, journalist *Hedrick Smith:* "I have read your story, 'Christmas Eve 1927,' and I enjoyed it. You have a nice, easy, lean writing style that graphically portrays the out of doors and animals, and especially the chill of the Christmas season in 1927 . . . . [The fact] that this story which you shared with me was the result of long practice . . . shows. You are a craftsman."

Basketball great *Bill Sharman:* "Many thanks for sharing such a wonderful story with me. It was *great!*!!"

Former Secretary of Energy *James Edwards:* "You obviously have a real talent for writing . . . . Your descriptions were wonderful. Your father, Dr. Weber, was certainly an outstanding man . . . and I wish we had physicians like him today . . . . [He was] made of sterner stuff and had a more compassionate heart and a more generous soul than we have in our professions now."

Dr. James S. Todd, Executive Vice President of the American Medical Association: "I thoroughly enjoyed the story about your physician father. Your ending was just perfect . . . . [You] tell a great story!"

Legendary football star *Elroy "Crazy Legs" Hirsch:* *"Great* story! Be proud."

Richard G. Kleindienst, former Attorney General: "You write well . . . [and] are justifiably proud of your father."

Singer *Carol Lawrence:* "You are an amazingly sensitive man . . . . What a blessing your father must be to inspire such enduring love from you! Thanks for sharing a small glimpse of his soul with me. I was moved to sweet tears."

Dr. Michael E. DeBakey, famed heart surgeon: "Thank you for . . . the story about your father. It is a beautiful story of a dedicated physician and a fine tribute to your father. He exemplifies . . . [those] physicians through the ages who chose the medical profession because they truly wanted to help patients get well and who made many personal sacrifices without regard for personal gain [to do so]."

Comedian *Dick Martin:* "Your story about your father was very good."

Actress *Lizabeth Scott:* "What a wonderful man Dr. J. P. Weber was! You *should* be very proud of him . . . . I read your story 'Christmas Eve 1927.' It is emotionally touching. You are an excellent writer."

Judith Crist, movie critic: "Your . . . letter with the lovely story about your father was lost behind a filing cabinet. We just moved the file this week and found it. What a charming story to have about one's parent! You are a lucky man."

Actress *Rita Gam:* "Thank you for sharing your very moving Christmas story with me. I received it on a hot summer's day. It was a welcome breath of air. You write very well."

Julie Nixon Eisenhower: "The short story about your father was beautiful. His character reminded me a great deal of my mother's early years in Artesia, California. The doctor who cared for her mother during her terminal illness was a country doctor like your father. But the dedication and devotion to duty and to healing was extraordinary in your father's case. I think your father would have been very proud of the story."

Actress *Jane Wyatt:* "I was so very interested in your Dr. Weber's story . . . . [He] was certainly a very great fellow!"

Model *Cheryl Tiegs:* "Thanks for sending the wonderful story . . . . [It is] very inspirational."

Actor *Art Carney:* "I thoroughly enjoyed the story you wrote about your father."

Actor *Karl Malden:* "Tom—a wonderful story!"

Actor *Robert Culp:* "I did enjoy your story—more than you will ever know. Thank you for letting me read it."

Elizabeth Dole: "It is a story of a brave man's selflessness, skill, and determination to make a positive difference in the lives of others. That is a valuable legacy which will guide you during the years ahead and bring continuing honor to your family."

The beloved actress *Patricia Neal:* "Thank you so much for sending me this fantastic letter. The stories of your father, Dr. Weber, were absolutely fascinating. What an incredible man he was. If I were a man, I would love to play him on the screen."

Connie Chung: "I really appreciate your telling me about your father. What a wonderful man he was!"

Ranulph Fiennes, who is generally regarded as the world's greatest living explorer: "Many thanks for your interesting stories about Dr. Weber . . . . [He was] an amazing character."

Actress *Estelle Parsons:* "What inspiration! Thank you. It lives in the telling."

xxx

Television personality *Ed McMahon:* "What an incredible story, and what a magnificent life. He truly exemplifies man's indomitable spirit and how that can reflect itself in great charitable deeds. It should be that when you look up 'Good Samaritan' in the dictionary, there would be a picture of your father, Dr. Weber."

Former Watergate Special Prosecutor *Archibald Cox:* "The Christmas story about your father, Dr. J.P. Weber, is very moving. I am glad to have had a chance to read it."

Actress *Jane Greer:* "I certainly was moved by the story of your dad. How proud you must be, having a legacy of tenderness and love from such a caring human being. You write very well. The trip was especially real and harrowing. Thanks for sharing it with me. I'll keep it, gladly."

Olympic Champion diver *Micki King:* "Thank you so much for writing to me and especially for sharing the story of your father's amazing medical practice. It is truly inspiring to hear about people who make doing the right thing the highest priority in their lives. I turned the pages . . . as though I were reading an exciting historical novel. My compliments on your story telling ability, and I do hope you have begun a written history of your father's brilliant acts of heroism, as future generations are sure to be moved by this dedicated and inspirational man . . . . My hope is that you will use your writing talents to convey to children the lessons your father taught you about helping others and showing kindness and compassion to those who are less fortunate. We need more heroes like your father."

Joan Rivers: "Thank you, thank you, thank you so much for taking the time and trouble to send me your great letter . . . . Your father sounds like he was a wonderful and caring man. If only there were doctors today like him."

Singer *Peggy Lee:* "What a hero your father was! Or even a saint."

Actress *Betty Garrett:* "I loved your story about your father."

Actress *Gale Storm:* "What a wonderful, thrilling letter telling of your father's life of goodness and mercy!"

Actor *Tony Randall:* "Beautiful story, Tom."

Actress *Rita Moreno:* "What a lovely story! What a wonderful father! You must be so proud."

Thomas Carper, former Governor of Delaware: "Thank you for taking the time to write and include the story you wrote about your father. I thoroughly enjoyed the story and its encouraging message. Your father sounds like a very unique man. He viewed his profession as more than an occupation. His compassion toward others and his willingness to brave horrendous conditions to bring warmth and love to others reflects a rare quality of empathy."

Olympic track champion, *Joan Benoit:* "Thanks so much for sharing your father's story with me. He certainly was a hard-working, dedicated, talented, selfless and inspiring man. A true pioneer in the field of medicine . . . . No case was too challenging in his eyes. Dr. J.P. Weber's life and the accounts of his practice should be required reading for all medical students. And to think that doctors think they have it tough these days."

Former Senator *George McGovern:* "Thank you for . . . the fascinating story about your father, Dr. J.P. Weber."

Pete Rozelle, former Commissioner of the National Football League: "I . . . certainly enjoyed receiving the beautiful, descriptive story about your father, Dr. Weber."

Actress *Carol Alt:* "Your dad was a very special person. A saint . . . . I was very impressed. Nowadays doctors don't even make house calls. You should be very proud."

Actress *Joan Fontaine:* "Thank you for allowing me to read about . . . [your father]. What a marvelous human being."

Actress *Hazel Court:* "I loved your story. Thank you so much for sending it to me. A story to warm the heart. I wish there were more like him today."

Robert MacNeil, television news commentator: "Your story about your father's Christmas ride in Idaho long ago is very moving."

Harvey Cox, Dean of the Harvard Divinity School: "Thanks for the great story!"

Actress *May Britt:* "Your story about your father is very compelling. Thank you for sending it!"

Actress *Stella Stevens:* "Thank you for your wonderful . . . story of Dr. Weber. I have kept . . . [it] filed away so I can look at it for inspiration every now and then."

Pollster *Lou Harris:* "I am moved by your words."

Tennis great *John Newcombe:* "I loved your little story and the message it carried."

Vince Dooley, football coach and athletic administrator: "I thoroughly enjoyed reading the story about your father. It did indeed carry a profound message and was quite moving."

Actor *Robert Stack:* "A very interesting, touching story."

Frederick Dent, former Secretary of Commerce: "Your story of Christmas 1927 describes the very best in the spirit of Americans as well as of the Christmas season. What a heritage your father has left you."

Actress *Beverly Garland:* "What a lovely Christmas story!"

Actress *Maureen Stapleton:* "The story was beautiful. What a wonderful man. Thank you!"

Actress *Samantha Eggar:* "It is an human endearing story. Thank you for allowing me to read it. Thank God for those who care."

Actress *Dorothy Provine:* "Thank you so much for sending me the story you wrote about your father. He must have been a marvelous man! You wrote his story with great sensitivity. It was a privilege to read it and I thank you for sending it to me."

Singer *Gloria Loring:* "Your story is lovely, filled with the love and respect you have for your father."

Football Coach *Bobby Bowden:* "Thanks very much for your note and especially the story 'Christmas Eve 1927.' Once I got started I couldn't put it down, although I was in a hurry to go catch a plane. That was an excellent story and shows you how much this country has changed in the last 65 years. Boy, what a man your dad was. I know where he is today."

Writer *William Peter Blatty:* "I like 'Christmas Eve 1927' very much. Your father was a wonderful man."

Bob Bergland, former Secretary of Agriculture: "Thanks for . . . this moving story about your father—'Christmas Eve 1927.' He was a remarkable person. Thanks to you for recording one of his many unusual experiences."

Writer *Perri Klass:* "Thank you for letting me see this story, and for thinking I would appreciate it, which I did. I must say, I think it is a wonderful way to remember and pay tribute to your father, and to his life, and even his landscape. The story succeeds really well as a portrait of a life, a beautiful and terrible natural setting, and a beautiful and terrible moment in the Qualey house."

Gwendolyn Brooks, poet and writer: "Thank you so much . . . for your father's story, which I considered honestly written, interesting, and very sensitive to the positives of this world. Thank you, truly."

C. Douglas Dillon, former Secretary of the Treasury: "Thank you for letting me see the story about your father. It is very moving. Your father was a truly great man. I wish there were more like him in public life today."

Actress *Elaine Stewart:* "I read with pleasure your 'Christmas Eve 1927.' It is beautiful and moving and you should be very proud of what you have written. Your dad, Dr. Weber, was really a marvelous human being—so caring and kind. The world needs more people like him. Just the thought of what he went through to get to Mrs. Qualey to let her know that somebody cares! He must have been much adored—a man with a great soul . . . . Stay with the good writing. I'm keeping it of course, and I'm sure I'll read it again."

Actor *Martin Sheen:* "Thank you so much for . . . the beautiful story of your father's journey—'Christmas Eve 1927'! What an extraordinary story about an extraordinary man! Congratulations to you for writing such a fine remembrance."

Ben Bradlee, former editor of the Washington *Post:* "That story is written just fine, better than just fine. Thank you for sending it to me. He must have been quite a man."

David Cargo, former Governor of New Mexico: "This is truly a beautiful story and it is extremely well done. I must say that this is the work of a professional writer. I am indeed impressed."

McGeorge Bundy, former U.S. Cabinet member: " . . . [Your story] carries quite a message. I have indeed enjoyed reading it and this note brings my thanks for it. It will help me remember that it's important for all sorts of people to get good evidence that 'somebody cares.' Thanks again."

To my father

CHAPTER ONE

Peter Weber was trained as a butcher in Germany, but when he and his wife, Augusta, and their five children immigrated to the town of Creston in southwestern Iowa in 1885, he found work as a railroad laborer. Forty-three when he arrived in the United States, the short, hard-working man had a reputation for being thoroughly honest.

Highly intelligent and deeply spiritual, Augusta Menard Weber came from a family which owned a porcelain factory in Berlin. With blue, flashing eyes and smooth straw-colored hair, she was a beautiful woman. Augusta was a happy person, one who frequently burst into gay laughter and who could quickly charm even the most withdrawn of neighbors.

On Monday, May 14, 1888, the forty-four-year-old Augusta gave birth to John Peter at the Weber home on Elm Street in Creston.

Little Johnny's world was filled with the wonder of the many stories and recollections related by his

1

mother. Every seam on her face held the key to a new and exciting remembrance. How lovely she seemed to Johnny! How talented, how all-knowing, how warm! Never would he forget her captivating smile, her wonderful creamy arms reaching out to embrace him.

One afternoon during the Fall of 1899, Johnny busily loaded canned fruit into the family cellar. As he stopped to rest, he sighted the town physician, Dr. Claybaugh, passing in a fine carriage, his dark suit impeccable, his black brimmed hat straight and proud on his gray-haired head. Johnny's mother had often spoken of the spring day in 1888 when Dr. Claybaugh came to the house to deliver him.

The old doctor cracked his whip over the flanks of the smartly galloping team, no doubt hurrying to a patient who desperately needed him. The air filled with the rattle of wheels on the sturdy brick road.

Leaning against the side of the house to watch, Johnny whispered to himself, "Someday I'm going to be a doctor."

After finishing the eighth grade, John, now five feet four inches tall and weighing 135 pounds, heard that men were being hired to construct railroad tracks across Montana and that the wages were good.

Unable to afford a ticket, he decided to ride the rails hobo-style to the western state.

The young man soon learned there were difficulties with riding in boxcars. The conductors and brakemen who patrolled the freight trains always demanded money—ten cents, a quarter, sometimes half a dollar— or they kicked you off.

The alternative was riding the rods, the two narrow steel beams beneath a passenger car. But riding on the "lower berth" had its problems too. Hanging onto the rods with his forearms and legs, keeping his eyes shut to avoid the hot blinding cinders, John soon felt exhaustion setting in. It was all a fellow could do just to hold on, with the roadbed only inches below his back. And you didn't know how long it would be between stops.

At North Platte, a brakeman saw John duck under a car and stretch out on the rods just as the train was beginning to roll. He ran alongside the train cursing John's ancestry, pelting him with rocks as long as he could, but the young man was able to hold on.

That evening, the train was going at quite a clip when it began a twisting roller-coaster ride through the mountains. John's car was rolling and swaying like a ship in a storm as it tore down the hooking track.

Jackrabbits scurried off in the dark at the side of the railbed, rattlesnakes jerked and wheeled away from the train.

John fought the force of the curves, his body jolting precariously with the motion of the train, wind swelling his clothes like sails. Cinders burned holes in his pants, grasshoppers and bugs filled his mouth and eyes and shirt while the knife-edged wheel buzzed at his arm.

The massive car pitched down the side of a mountain, shooting around the curves. Someone was calling for brakes while the brakeman yelled that the brakes were frozen. Then, as morning dawned, the train squealed deafeningly to a halt, and John rolled out from under the car to gaze at a glorious cathedral of trees. Someone said it was Montana.

It was a harsh land, one where the wind sometimes brought seasonal changes so suddenly that snow poured down on the open blossoms of lilac trees. For months John labored in all kinds of weather, saving most of his money.

Dressed in overalls, John was one of the graders whose job it was to build and level an elevated roadbed. Immense amounts of dirt had to be shoveled to make the grade while cuts had to be hacked out of hills with picks to make the roadbed level. Only the hardiest of workers could sustain a long day of digging and moving dirt and rock.

Once a section of railbed was completed and the ties laid, John and two other workmen would pick up a thirty-foot section of rail using tongs and drop it in place on the ties. Each rail weighed 560 pounds. Spikers with sledgehammers drove seven-inch spikes into the ties to hold the rails in place.

The railroad construction workers lived in tents. Each morning they filed into a large tent that served as a mess hall and arranged themselves along a lengthy table. The front line of men then sat on a bench before tin plates that were nailed to the tabletop. An attendant walked alongside the table and sloshed a meal of meat, beans and potatoes onto each plate from a large pot while the hungry men picked up their forks and quickly devoured it. When finished, they filed out of the mess hall and the server, carrying a bucket of water and an old mop, swabbed out the plates and dipped the forks, filthy with incrustations dark and deep, briefly into the pail. Each succeeding line of "diners" was so famished it ignored all concerns for sanitation and quickly devoured their portion of goulash as it was slopped onto their plates. The procedure was repeated at noon and each evening.

John's foreman, George, had served as an infantry commander in Puerto Rico during the Spanish-American War. Over six feet tall and possessing an iron demeanor, he used physical force as his primary managerial tool. George would walk up and down the line barking orders at the sweating workmen, brandishing an ax handle, making no allowances for human frailties. Apparently no one had told him the war was over.

One day the men were hard at work, rhythmically swinging picks and shovels, engraving a necklace of steel across the State of Montana. George suddenly pulled out a pistol and began snapping slugs at the heels of a man he considered a laggard. Another time, he used his bullwhip on the backside of a worker who was loitering.

Men sometimes collapsed from heat stroke or dehydration. There were days when rattlesnakes were so thick the men spent more time killing them than laying track. Working on the railroad was good survival training—if you made it through the course.

George always wore dark funereal clothes. There was the hint of a long-forgotten part in his lengthy black hair. It may have even been fully combed at one time. The grave foreman seldom gave the hint of a smile, but when he did it was only a short time until the habitual furrows of disgust got his face back under control. Whenever he got down to inspect the men's work it looked like nothing so much as a long cockroach crawling between the tracks.

Tree stumps and large rocks had to be cleared from the roadway. Because of his exceptional dexterity, John was chosen to drill holes in them and insert blasting powder. Although he appreciated being honored for his steady hands, the young man found tamping explosives into rocks with a crowbar and igniting the fuses to be a rather frightening business.

One evening early in October, John sat in his tent after supper and took off his boots. His feet were blistered and bleeding. Red tributaries crossed the divides of his toes and trickled to the floor.

The temperature had dropped below freezing. George opened the flap of the tent and announced that the rail gang would be laying track until midnight. He didn't sound in a mood to excuse anyone from work.

A gale-force wind razored through the mountain passes. Even the rocks on top of the railbed were moving. Dirt-caked men labored without speaking in the eerie glow of lanterns and guttering torches.

George stalked the grade, spitting out orders, his narrow face crimson with cold, his hair rimed with ice. He was really crazy tonight, out of control, roaring at times with rage.

John forced himself to perform the grinding, monotonous pick-and-shovel toil, panting, sobbing, finally slumping to the ground in exhaustion, the pick slipping from his frozen hands. General George saw him attempting to start a little fire to warm his hands, and began hitting him with a club.

That night, John collapsed into his bedroll, rubbing his bruises, weeping. He had a thought, brought it out and examined it. He turned it over and looked at the underside. No worrisome fins or scales were evident. Early the next morning he started hiking westward.

CHAPTER TWO

The highest chimney of the town's smelter went up like a great darkened vase above the huddled houses. Mining operations on the hill had smoked everything into a brown dinginess. Even the sky looked as if it had come out of the stacks.

Storefronts on each side of Granite Street looked like worn playing cards stuck into the dirt. Some of them weren't saloons.

John's left foot came out of the manure with a loud "sock-sock-sock." Around the corner swung a large brewery wagon pulled by four horses, nearly burying him in a moving wall of slop. Welcome to Butte.

The sidewalks were somewhat varied. Planks thrown carelessly across mudholes in some places, they were full boardwalks in others. Many of them tilted dangerously sideways on inclines, but mostly they were non-existent.

Getting across intersections took enterprise, with running livestock often crowding the road. Oxen wallowed belly-high in the soupy mire while burly men wrestled barrels and crates from wagons onto dry land.

Clusters of streetlamps tried but failed to penetrate the swirling smoke, even at midday. Lanterns or torches were carried by some wary pedestrians. John worked his way up the sidewalk toward a barber shop not by what he saw but by following the hacking cough of his forerunner.

The place was crowded with miners waiting for a haircut. John took a seat on the corpse of a sofa and pulled a sheet of paper from his pocket. Spiders and roaches stalked across the floor while bugs buzzed a symphony around his head.

Red-eyes miners sat wheezing, snorting, sneezing and sniffling. Their coughs barely shook the windows. The room resounded with talk of cave-ins, fires, black lung, cage falls, and rocks landing on miners' heads. Waiting his turn, John penned a letter to his parents, warning his mother of the envelope that nothing crawl out.

His hair stylist may not have graduated first in his class from barber school. The large jug-eared man liked to take nips of bourbon while he worked. By the time John escaped the palsied coiffeur he wasn't sure whether he'd had a haircut or surgery.

He picked his way up the boardwalk through the choking ether. Every man he saw was armed. Some looked like walking arsenals.

The bulk of a large building loomed out of the murk to his right. He squinted into the smoke. There was a sign on the front.

He drew the sleeve of his jacket across his eyes to wipe away a layer of brown film. Blinking, he moved closer until he could make out the sign: "Mining Jobs."

In the center of the structure was a doorway. John stepped toward it and turned the knob. Hinges creaked as the door opened.

He stepped inside, letting his eyes adjust to the cavelike darkness of a hallway. Something small scurried across his shoe.

John's footsteps thumped their way down the hall. Just around a corner, an old codger wallowed on a bench, spitting tobacco, his features partially hidden in shadow. Reading John's mind before he could say anything, he motioned over his shoulder with a thumb like an umpire signaling a runner out. John hurried up the flight of stairs the man had gestured toward.

A long counter crossed the heart of the office. A few feet behind it hung a pale curtain.

John tapped a bell on the counter and waited, looking up at the water-stained ceiling. Outside the window, smoke streamed from the seven stacks on the hill.

He rang the bell again. No one was home. Hiring offices could be as slow as a girl getting ready for a date and just as full of excuses.

There was the sound of footsteps. A shadow clawed at the curtain. The cloth parted and the shadow became a tall man with a long brown beard that was crimped as though he'd been sleeping on it.

"Name's O'Farrell. What can I help you with, boy?"

"Mr. O'Farrell, I am looking for work. I helped lay the tracks across—"

"Where you from, boy?"

"A little town in Iowa named Creston, sir."

The man slumped into an easy chair. The remnants of a recent meal nestled in his beard. His eyebrows could have been used as whiskbrooms.

"Well, what do you think of our fair city, boy?"

John hesitated. "Well, sir, I haven't seen enough of it to decide." He was lying. He had.

"To tell you the truth, boy, mining is a great career. There's a wide variety of jobs. You could be a nipper. Them's the guys that take supplies down into the mine. You could be a mucker. You could help pull cinders out of the furnace."

A loud whistle blew. John looked out the window. Across the street, a shift had ended. Mud-smeared miners bubbled up from the cages.

A well-missed spittoon sat in a corner of the room. The hiring officer turned his head to one side and spat a long stream of tobacco in its general direction, then wiped his lips with the back of his hand.

This was some job interview. "Yeah, boy, we pay good. You'll never have an empty lunch pail." O'Farrell gagged and spat another stream of tobacco juice. "Beats shoveling horse manure in the street."

Things were moving in his wildlife-habitat beard. "There's plenty culture in this town, boy. We've got dog racing, horse racing. Some of the taverns have rooster fights. Of course, during winter you'll have to buy your whisky by the chunk."

The man began cackling ridiculously. His breath constituted a threat to the neighborhood.

"Mr. O'Farrell, what qualifications do I have to have to work here?"

O'Farrell turned and spat a tangled mass of brown fiber and juice toward the spittoon. This time it actually went in, landing with a sickening plop.

"Well, the only thing young boys like you have to do is prove they can handle a little Michigan Hay." He pulled a chaw of fine cut from his shirt pocket and stuck it at John.

Backing away from the counter, John said, "Well, sir, I'll have to think about it." As the young man walked from the room, Mr. Clean resumed his insane cackling.

John walked down the stairs into the hallway. He felt unclean. The old man was still lounging on his bench. Staring at John, he grinned. Tobacco juice ran down his cheek knowingly.

John groped his way through the dark corridor toward the door. The caps and overalls of miners hung from hooks on the wall, like the bodies of men.

John headed down a walkway that was splintery and wobbly, smoke searing his throat. Loud music from a dance hall filled the air.

A patch of color darker than the mist moved up the street toward him. A breeze made haze waver in front of him, and the figure split into two blobs moving side by side, then merged back into one.

Fascinated, John stopped, letting the swimming sensation pass. He noticed he had just walked past a bank.

There was the liquid swish of a silk dress on boards that were broken and rotting. Two feminine boots penetrated the thick vapor, boots fit for proper paving.

The blob slowly resolved itself into a gorgeous blue gown trimmed with sparkling jewels, then the comely lines of a stunning figure. Coral cheeks against a dark edge of fur spoke eloquently of youth and health. Mounds of soft ashen hair swayed behind perfect red lips and a graceful neck. A dainty derringer was slung to the charming waist.

Mouth wide open, John stared. She was slightly bent over, clutching the tops of her stockings which were full of silver dollars.

The young woman smiled at him. "Honey," she said, "come over to the *Pay Day* in a few minutes and buy me a drink." Then the radiant face moved past him, disappearing in the cold smoke.

The boardwalk soon ended and John moved into the street, pushing his legs through knee-deep mud. People and animals meandered their way through the muck ahead of him, gradually taking on the color of the road. It got so the only way he could distinguish a living creature from the mire was movement.

Slogging a course around yellowish puddles that reeked of urine, John passed a livery stable, a Chinese washee-washee house, a general store. To his left, children in their patched clothes peeked under the batwing doors of a saloon into a forbidden grownup world.

It was becoming quite dark as he approached the outskirts of town. A thin scrap of moon hung in a gap of the mountains like a lemon slice in a tall drink. John drew a bead on the Big Dipper and headed for the handle. The thrill of hopping a chugging train on a hill had become alluring to him.

CHAPTER THREE

The tracks appeared in the moonlight. John heard the great iron horse before he saw it, a laboring moan out of the darkness, then the familiar clicking of wheels on the cold iron rails. The headlight swayed through the trees like a lantern, the engine shuddering like a large beast.

The speed of the locomotive slackened on the steep grade until the wheels groaned against the tracks. As soon as the engine passed, the youngster began to run along the cinders, watching for his chance.

He spied a boxcar and jumped straight at it, grabbing the handrail and quickly vaulting to the stirrups. Listening to the wheels pound below, he stood straddling the space between the cars, one foot in the stirrup of the car he had just grabbed, the other on the car behind. Directly below was the rushing roadbed. He leaped upward, grasped the edge of the roof and muscled his way toward the top as the train lurched in the darkness, a desperate maneuver on the now accelerating train. At length, he reached the roof of the car and lay down in exhaustion.

Later, the train headed across a trestle which spanned a mighty canyon, rotten timbers groaning and swaying below. The car rocked from side to side, sliding John this way and that on the ice-covered roof, threatening to hurl his freezing body off into the night.

At last, the train reached the end of the trestle. Quaking with cold and other things, the young man stared upward, breathing heavily. A sharp wind whipped his eyes so that the stars above seemed to burst into brilliant streamers.

Next morning, the train shot with a deafening roar into the darkness of a tunnel that seemed to have no end. The clamor of the cars was almost unendurable and John grew dizzy as engine fumes engulfed him. Consciousness barely flickered in him when, suddenly, light struck his eyes and the horrible din diminished to a muffled cadence. Fresh air quickly filled his lungs. He rose to a sitting position, blinked his eyes and looked back at the exit of the tunnel glowering like the eye socket of a charred skull.

Portland, Oregon, on the banks of the Columbia River, sat this October day in 1904 among lush forests, mountains and cliffs. The main street was a sweep of wagon-channeled black mud, a tumult of drays, carriages and buggies driven at ridiculous speeds while men on horseback darted in and out of the traffic. It was every driver for himself.

Wearing his work boots, a new pair of pants, a nicely stitched Western shirt and a blue jacket, John strode through the drizzly town, the hollow boardwalk amplifying his footsteps as if they were being struck on a big drum.

He passed bearded, brawny loggers carrying their bindles, or tied-up belongings, as they strolled the muddy streets and wooden sidewalks. These men were dressed in heavy, spike-soled boots, wool shirts, and tin pants, which were tight around the ankles and covered with pitch and dirt. They had come out of the forest to rest and "go down to splash"—get drunk—before beginning another hard month in the mountain logging camps.

John saw a rugged lumberjack standing in front of a restaurant and went over to talk to him.

"Say, sir, do you know of any logging jobs that are available?"

"No, lad, I sure don't," replied the logger, shaking his head. "The lumber business usually slows down at this time of year and then starts up again real heavy in the spring. Fact is, I just lost my job a couple days ago myself."

"Oh, I'm sorry to hear that, sir." John tipped his hat and walked on.

The young man from Iowa soon fell victim to a pickpocket as he made his way through a jostling crowd on a street corner. He wandered the city streets for weeks, looking for a job, surviving only be eating daily at a soup kitchen for the homeless on Burnside Street. Barren tree branches poked the sky with gray fingers that warned of winter.

Every now and then he was arrested on charges of vagrancy. The police would throw him into a horse-drawn paddy wagon in which a little mountain of twisted bodies heaved and tossed against each other.

One night, as he languished on the jailhouse floor, his earnest blue eyes innocent and glowing, one of the inmates asked him what he wanted to be "when you grow up."

"Oh," replied John, lifting his head from the floor and propping his chin up with a fist, "I'm going to be a doctor." The other men inside the cell roared with laughter at the absurdity of a bum becoming a doctor.

During the afternoon of Saturday, December seventeenth, sixteen-year-old John Weber worked his way down a street in Portland, hoping he could make it to the food wagon. After a time, he leaned against a storefront to rest. Bustling crowds passed, laughing faces with breath visible in the cold, arms carrying gaily wrapped packages. He stared into the faces. None looked back at him.

He began to walk again. It was difficult to stay upright. Presently, a group of well-dressed men approached. John didn't see them in time to get out of the way and one of them, a tall, long-faced dandy in a brown derby hat, shoved him rudely off the wooden sidewalk. He fell on his back in the gutter full of slush and rocks. The men continued onward while one said something about John and the rest burst out laughing.

Slowly, John regained his feet and staggered in the general direction of the meal wagon, pain shooting up his back.

He hobbled over to where the wagon stood, the pressure of the line of other ragged men holding him up and moving him forward.

The countertop was set up. John got his food, then lay on the ground, drinking soup and munching bread. The wind blew his flimsy jacket open at the front. He began to cough spasmodically. It hurt deep in his chest.

A heavy, icy rain spurted down from the gloomy sky. Drenched, skeletal cats prowled around, rubbing their hips and tails against him, searching for crumbs.

Someone was standing over him. She was covered in green, her cotton dress flared, sashed at the waist and to the ankles. The young woman's eyes were blue, friendly over a smile of white.

She bent over him, her dark-green cape open, the brim of her floppy hat touching the top of his head. She studied his eyes, the blue irises nearly swallowing the pupils and shining with illness.

"Young man," she asked, "what is your name?"

John tried to think, but he couldn't remember. He looked away, making no reply. His face was pale, the cheeks chapped from the cold, his lips blistered. His hair was long and dirty, sticking out in all directions and over his ears.

She tugged at his arm. "Why don't we walk down the street together?" she offered, then helped him stand. "Come and have supper with me. Come, young man, please come."

A wave of vertigo swept over him as he stood, bent over like an old man. He looked down at his frayed trousers, stiff with filth, and at last mumbled, "John."

She helped him walk along the sidewalk. He dropped to a knee from time to time, his feet nearly frozen, his lips moving as if he were speaking, but no sound coming out.

They entered an apartment house and slowly climbed the carpeted stairs. At length, a small lamp illuminated one of the doors, and she opened the latch.

"We'll have supper in a minute," she said, settling him in a chair. She lit the gas stove burners with a long match. "But first you'll have to take a bath," she insisted, smiling.

She showed him to the bathroom and started the water in the oval porcelain tub, then left.

John slowly disrobed and lay in the water, amazed at the simple feeling of warmth and comfort. He thought of his tattered, filthy clothes, regretting that he would have to put them on again, then noticed she had set an old, but patched and clean, pile of clothes on a chair by the door.

After awhile, when the water had cooled somewhat, he climbed out of the tub, dried himself and put on the clothes. Shaving himself in front of the mirror was a shocking experience because he could clearly see how much his appearance had deteriorated.

He limped out of the bathroom and gazed around. A colorful Christmas tree stood in a corner, about four feet tall. There weren't any fancy ornaments, just shiny red apples suspended by threads, and many lighted candles of various colors in small metal holders clipped to the branches. A few colorfully wrapped packages sat at the base of the tree near a nativity scene whose clay figures gazed into the manger.

Wearing an apron over her lovely flowered dress, the young lady was placing food on the table, her dishwater blonde hair brushed neatly back, a wide furrow extending from her forehead to the bun at the nape of her neck.

They sat at the table and she offered a loving prayer over the food, graciously thanking God for sending John to visit her. There was soup containing vegetables, meat and noodles, a far cry from the pitiful rice water he had been getting at the wagon. There were homemade biscuits, cubed steak and mashed potatoes smothered with butter. A small buttercake lay on the sideboard, ready for slicing.

John gulped down his milk, grabbed a couple of pieces of steak with his fingers and popped them into his mouth. He lifted the bowl of soup with both hands, ready to slurp it like an animal as he had for so long at the wagon. The lovely young woman picked up a spoon from the table and looked at him, smiling.

He ate in complete silence, overwhelmed by his incredible fortune, still wondering whether it was real. When he had eaten all he could, he raised his hollow face from his meal.

"Do you feel better now, John?" the young woman asked.

He nodded. "What is your name, ma'am?"

"I'm Nancy Jacobsen. I'm a nurse," she said, folding her napkin neatly on the table. Strangely, she didn't seem to fear him, a stranger. He felt that she was a brave soul.

"Well, Miss Jacobsen," he said weakly, "you're a wonderful lady and I am truly grateful for this meal." He rose from his chair, stiff and feeble from illness. "I'll be going now. I sleep under the bridge. I can probably—"

"You will sleep here," Nancy said firmly. She got up and led him to a little cot covered with fresh flannel sheets, a homemade quilt of many squares and colors, and an inviting pillow wearing a clean white slip.

Astounded, John lay across the cot, burying his head in a pillow for the first time in weeks. A sudden gust of wind blew outside as rain spattered against a window pane. He shivered.

"If you need anything, just—"

"But, why, Nancy? Why are you being so kind to me?"

Nancy explained that she believed in helping the poor, it was part of her religion. "And I, well, I've been noticing you the last few days down at the soup wagon," she said, blushing slightly. "I feel you have potential."

"What—"

"Don't worry, John," she interrupted. "Just do something for someone else someday. That's all you have to do to repay me." She turned to go.

"I will," he whispered. He thought of all the men who would spend the night under the bridge, and pulled the soft blankets up to his chin. A carriage passed by on the street below. The clatter of wheels and hoofs on cobblestones reminded him vaguely of something from the past, something he had seen from the steps of the family cellar.

CHAPTER FOUR

Professor Kasimir Zurawski looked up at the sharply slanting lecture hall filled with freshman students, a few of whom were women. His heavily bearded face and petite granny glasses made him like an intelligent werewolf.

"Ladies and gentlemen," he declaimed loudly, "please look at the student seated on your right. Now look at the one on your left. Don't get too well acquainted because one of the three of you will not graduate."

Dressed in a blue suit, twenty-four-year-old John Weber chuckled nervously with his new classmates. He thought of the many years he had spent working on the railroad in Iowa in order to complete his undergraduate education, and of his recent train trip to Chicago, the first he'd made while seated in a passenger car.

"Loyola University is a great institution," declared the professor, almost shouting, his beard jerking vigorously up and down, then side to side. John knew that Professor Zurawski was a brilliant man who had graduated with high honors from the University of Illinois Medical Department.

"You will receive a splendid education here. But remember that medicine is a challenging profession. It will be necessary that you work long hours, that you serve the rich and the poor alike." He paused, fiddling with his spectacles. "That is, if you graduate."

The laughter wasn't as loud this time.

The professor's eyes grew stern. "Now pick a cadaver and start dissecting!" There was a buzzing surge as students spilled into the aisles.

The dissecting room was powerfully illuminated by overhead lights. Water trickled in a trough around the edge of the cement floor. On the left side of the room, several skeletons hung on chains, turning slowly in the air.

At the back of the room was the freezer where cadavers were stored. The frozen bodies hung from the ceiling on tongs, grotesque, misshapen, females mixed with males, the young and the old suspended in the equality of death. A lightbulb at the rear of the compartment cast distorted shadows on the ceiling, floor and wall. Each student was obliged to walk through the eerie freezer, bumping from time to time against a variety of rigid extremities.

After removing his suit coat, John chose the corpse of an old man, took it down, washed it, laid it on a table and started pulling the skin off. Sweet smelling cadaver juice covered his instruments, his hands and, soon, even his hair. At the end of the day he draped the cadaver with a black oil cloth and left the dreadful room.

Within a few days he had dissected the muscle layers, tracing out the blood vessels and following the course of the nerves, knowing that by mid-term he would be required to recognize and name several thousand anatomical parts.

Not far from the school was the elevated railway, its huge iron underpinnings growing out of the street like black claws reaching for the sky. John, now five feet seven inches tall and weighing 145 pounds, boarded the train each afternoon at five-thirty and rode it to the LaSalle Street Railroad Station in downtown Chicago, carrying his textbooks with him. Dressed in rugged work clothes, the husky young man loaded and unloaded heavy express freight from six to midnight, for which he was paid twenty-five cents an hour. During a typical evening, the depot was a vast welter of confusion, filled with the noise of bells and whistles and voices, of trundling carts, of entering and departing trains.

Station platforms were heaped with wooden boxes and cartons from the trains. John lugged the packages onto flat wagons and, together with the other workmen, struggled with the larger pieces. The carts they pulled to waiting trucks and horse-drawn vehicles at the dock were loaded with a thousand pounds of goods, sometimes more.

Steam gushed from the wheels of the engines while smoke billowed from their smokestacks in black clouds, filling the station. There were running men, swinging lanterns, trains rumbling and squealing. Hulking railroad bullies stalked the depot, making sure the men were busy loading or unloading freight.

Between trains, John would grab a lantern and a medical book, hurry to a nearby packing box or piano case, look around quickly to see if a supervisor was watching, then lift the lid and crawl in, studying until he heard the sudden, ear-splitting howl of a train entering the depot.

By about ten o'clock each evening, John's clothes would grow heavy and soggy from the absorption of sweat from his body. He would remove them in the restroom and wring them out, then put them back on and return to work.

After the night's work was done, he rode the "el" to the station near the medical school and walked through the bleak alley behind his apartment house, finally collapsing into slumber on his bed. Milk wagons banged and clattered through the alley early each morning, waking him at just about the right time to get off to class.

John spent as much time as possible down the street at the Jefferson Park Hospital doing clinical work: examining patients and taking samples for laboratory work. Here the books he studied in packing boxes at the train station came to life. He learned the feel of the normal and the abnormal, the bumps, swellings, roughness, temperature, moistness. He found he had a knack for detecting the odors of disease in breath and skin, in sweat, pus and saliva.

John took the school year 1914-1915 off, working long hours each day at the LaSalle Street Station in order to have enough money to continue his education.

The excruciating years of loneliness, hunger, toil and study passed slowly. Sometimes John felt that a man stands alone in this world, a hungry, aching soul whose loneliness would surely drive him mad. But he steeled himself against the hardships of his life, enduring the cold and misery of his apartment, the long nights of labor at the railroad station, for he did not feel he was destined for failure.

One night he finished work at the railroad station and shuffled his way to the elevated train stop, exhausted from an evening of lifting and pulling heavy freight and intermittently studying while crouched in a piano case. His dungarees, soaked with sweat, steamed in the cold air, then stiffened with frost.

Clutching the textbooks to his chest, he stood awaiting the arrival of the train. A Windy City gale tried to blow him off the platform.

The express finally screetched into the station. Flopping heavily into a seat after paying his fare, John sighed. Depression rode his shoulders like an evil thing. He glanced to the right. Seated next to him was a shriveled old woman dressed in threadbare clothes. Between her legs she held a shoeshine box, her hands permanently stained by shoe blacking.

John's graduation exercises in 1917 were held at Orchestra Hall in downtown Chicago. After a series of lengthy faculty addresses mercifully ended, the rotund, mustachioed dean of the medical school, Dr.

Maximilian Herzog, strode to the center of the rostrum, his kindly eyes shiny in the bright lights. The new medics rose and joined him in reciting the ancient words of the Hippocratic Oath.

The dean read the names of the graduates alphabetically, his bushy mustache twitching as he spoke. John listened impatiently—"Joseph A. Stoeckinger, Nathan Swartz, R. Gillman Timms, George Ellsworth Turner, James J. Walsh, John Peter Weber."

As he walked across the stage to receive his diploma from the beloved dean, John smiled ruefully, remembering the night thirteen years earlier when a group of fellow prisoners lay on a jailhouse floor and laughed at him.

CHAPTER FIVE

With the entry of the United States into World War I in April 1917, John registered for the draft in Chicago. The Army Medical Corps actually had a surplus of volunteers, and he was never called to serve.

Dr. John Peter Weber interned at Oak Park Hospital, just outside of Chicago, then was hired to work as physician and surgeon at the Wabash Railroad Hospital in Peru, Indiana.

He married the lovely Marguerite Cassel in 1918 in Indiana. Because of Dr. Weber's love for the West, he and his wife moved to Wyoming in 1919.

Marguerite gave birth to two daughters, Jean and Lois. A baby boy died in infancy. Marguerite died tragically late in 1922 of typhoid fever.

A disconsolate Dr. Weber moved to Idaho in 1924, settling in Grangeville, the county seat of Idaho County. Grangeville lay amidst a beautiful farming region called Camas Prairie. A rugged plateau area, which included Joseph Plains, Doumecq Plains and

Horseshoe Bend, was situated to the west of the town. The Salmon River and its beautiful canyon extended from the southern boundary of Idaho County to the northern.

The Snake River and Oregon formed the western boundary of the county. The alpine Seven Devils Mountains and Hell's Canyon were located to the south of Grangeville.

East of the town stood a series of mountains extending into Montana. This wilderness area, part of the Bitterroot Mountain Range, was so primitive in Dr. Weber's day that much of it had not been surveyed. The southeastern portion of the county lay in the aptly named Primitive Area.

Dr. Weber married a beautiful nurse, Ida Mae Ells, in 1926. Ida was a wonderful, unselfish person. She had so much love for Dr. Weber that his life was much happier than before. Even his facial appearance seemed to change. Friends noticed a new look of nobility, wisdom, peace.

Ida Mae Ells

Early in the marriage, Dr. Weber bought a lovely piano. He and Ida would sit together and sing as they looked fondly into each other's eyes. When they sat at the dinner table, their hands would intertwine. "They were always holding hands," an old friend remembered in 1985. "They were truly in love."

Ida was an excellent mother to Dr. Weber's daughters by his earlier marriage. Jean and Lois were healthy, happy girls. Ida liked to dress them in bonnets and calf-length frocks of cotton and lace, their outfits complemented by white anklets and shiny slippers.

Ida was an ideal nurse. She cared about those the world had forgotten, didn't want or couldn't stand to look at. By all accounts, Dr. and Mrs. Weber constituted a marvelous medical team. Together they helped many people get well.

Ida took care of many of the practical aspects of Dr. Weber's medical business, such as bookkeeping and the completion of forms. Although she missed him greatly when he was away caring for patients, she encouraged him to continue the practice as a service to the people of the area.

Ruth

Dr. Weber drove to a town south of Grangeville early one spring to care for a sick man. Just as the patient was declared well and the doctor was getting ready to leave, the crank wall phone rang.

George, the father of Ruth Schafer, a girl of fourteen, was on the party line. The family lived at a farmhouse a few miles outside the town Dr. Weber was visiting.

Ruth had gone horseback riding that morning. There was thunder, and the horse reared up violently, throwing her from its back. She landed on a rusty pitchfork, which penetrated clear through her neck. George asked if Dr. Weber would come out immediately.

Unfortunately, the doctor's automobile wasn't working. Hastily, he checked around town, shivering from the chilly spring wind, but couldn't find anyone to give him a ride. He picked up his bag and started running.

After about a mile and a half, he came to a good-sized stream. The cold shock of stepping into the water made him catch his breath; still, he plunged forward, bag held high, driving his body through the water with a desperate energy. He must get there before the poor girl died.

Fortunately, there was a level gravel bottom to the river, for, long before he reached the middle, he was feeling the tug of the current. The water got deeper until it covered his stomach, so cold it made breathing difficult. Soon it reached to his upper ribs, pulling hard at him, trying to wash him downstream, his shoes now barely touching bottom.

Then came the intense cold as he moved up out of the water and began climbing the rocks that fringed the shore. His teeth chattered uncontrollably while his clothes stiffened in the wind. A numbness crept through his body.

But he ran, ran on, not caring that the ground was rocky and strewn with treacherous boulders. As he approached the house, he weaved from side to side like a long-distance runner at the end of an arduous race.

Ruth's sister, Janet, a red-haired freckled girl, sat in a corner, her knobby knees hiked to her chin. Seven years old, she was crying as she said her Rosary.

The aged priest, Father Davis, had hurried over from his nearby church. He was a rotund man with a large red-veined nose and a gray halo around his head for hair. Standing beside the bed, he opened a case, his hands quavering with age and sorrow. He placed a candle on a little table beside a worn wooden crucifix and lighted it.

The priest washed his thick hands in a bowl while he looked at the injured girl's closed eyes. "Holy Mary, mother of God," he intoned, "pray for us sinners now and at the hour of our death."

A few feet from the bed, George Schafer, a tall, broad-shouldered farmer, tried to comfort his work-worn wife, but she was delirious with grief.

Father Davis bowed his head and whispered, "Peace be to this house. You shall sprinkle me with hyssop, O Lord, and I shall be clean." His lips trembled as he spoke. "You shall wash me, and I will be whiter than snow."

Tears came into his eyes as he gazed at the girl's face, blameless, framed in long dark hair. "Go forth from this world, O Christian soul," he moaned, drawing a wool blanket over the bloodless face. As he was shutting his prayer book, there came a knock at the door.

The bereaved mother rose from her chair, wiping swollen eyes with her apron, and opened the door.

The short, husky man's face was covered with sweat and his clothes looked like they'd been drenched in a flood. "Hello, I'm Dr. Weber," he said breathlessly, tugging uncomfortably at wet pants that clung to his legs.

"Oh, I'm sorry we called you," said Mrs. Schafer, her voice unpleasantly high with hysteria. "I'm afraid Ruth is dead." There was a heavy resignation about her, as though she had signed an armistice with life before a shot could be fired. "We didn't know whether to call a doctor or an undertaker," she sighed, her tired face puckering with additional tears.

"Well, I'm sorry I took so long getting here, Mrs. Schafer." Stepping inside, the doctor nodded politely at the elderly priest and said, "Pardon me, Father." He paused, trying to catch his breath. Then his eyes brightened. "Well, let me take a look at her." As he shuffled across the room, he felt about half dead.

George embraced his wife. His large hands, which labored so hard to support his family, were knotted like the knots on a tree.

Dr. Weber pulled back the blanket. The girl's pulse was very weak. Her neck looked like a war zone. "Help me now," he whispered devoutly, trying not to show his consternation. Ruth's delicate features made him

41

think of Nancy Jacobsen at Portland. Suddenly, he was staggering through the muddy streets of the city, weak, hungry, nearly dead. His heart pounded.

Dr. Weber cleared Ruth's throat and mouth with his finger, then stuck a tube down her throat and blew into it. After a few minutes, she heaved, and blood poured out over her clothes.

Dr. Weber began to unbutton Ruth's blouse. Surprisingly, his hands were not trembling. Raindrops spattered against a window.

She was so petite, her skin so smooth, the drenched blouse slipped readily from her body. A tremendous feeling of warmth and purity was flowing through Dr. Weber's hands. Rain poured in a fury on the roof.

Her skin was white as silk, the breasts small and firm, tipped with pink innocence. But Ruth was falling, falling into a dark oblivion.

Little Janet held a candle for the doctor as he worked late into the night, repairing Ruth's throat and neck. Thunder bellowed, the windows rattled, the walls shook and the whole dark house periodically flared aglow with lightning. Still, there was a quiet authority present in the room.

Ruth was breathing regularly. Her pulse was stronger. Even her features had altered in some indefinable fashion for the better.

Quietly, Dr. Weber sat down on the bed beside her. He would save her. Through the days and nights ahead he would watch and tend her. He would breathe for her, if necessary, and feed her.

He took her young hand in his, felt a slight response. Thunder suddenly jolted the house with the ruthlessness of a mule's hind legs. The maidenly patient gasped. The yellow lightning of the lonesome Idaho wilderness flashed repeatedly.

The days immediately following Ruth's accident were excruciatingly difficult for her. In the matter of a moment, her young life had changed from activity and lightheartedness to pain and almost constant bed confinement. Her long, luxuriant hair, which she enjoyed so much, was now tied in a severe ponytail to keep it away from the injured area of her neck.

One afternoon, Ruth awoke from the drowsiness of pain medication and saw Dr. Weber sitting beside the bed. It had rained all that morning, and she felt exceptionally gloomy.

Her eyes filling with tears, Ruth picked up a notebook and poured her heart out to the doctor, describing fully her fears of permanent crippling and even death. Somehow sleep had become associated in her mind with drowning. Every time she felt herself approaching slumber, it frightened her terribly because she feared she would never wake up. She also wrote that she had long wanted to be a nurse and that now that dream appeared to be impossible.

Dr. Weber read her note. Then he took her hand in his. "I'm always here with you, Ruth," he said, "so you don't have to be afraid to go to sleep. I won't let anything bad happen to you."

His voice was firm. "I'm no prophet, don't pretend to be. But it is clear to me that you are a special young lady. Has it occurred to you that perhaps you have not yet completed all you were sent here to do? The pain and suffering you are now experiencing could well enhance your ability to give strength to others in their time of need. Maybe someday all this misery will seem worthwhile, or even important.

"When I worked at the railroad hospital in Peru, Indiana," he continued, "there were lots of times I felt down. I was just getting started as a doctor and some of the days could be pretty tough. Whenever

I got to feeling badly about things, I would sneak up to the fourth floor and visit a little three-year-old boy who had been born with a defective spine. He'd never known a day out of bed. I would pull a chair up beside his bed and read him a story. All the time I read to him, he wanted to hold my hand.

"Well, at first it seemed childish, you know, foolish, sitting there reading 'The Three Bears' or something. But after a while I began to understand why I did it. This crippled little boy was happier than I was.

"When I was finished reading and got up out of my chair, he always wanted me to stay. He would pull me down even though his entire hand barely fit around one of my fingers. He would give me a kiss on the cheek and make me promise to come back and see him soon. No matter how down I was when I went in there, I always left feeling sky high. I was beginning to realize the reason he was happy was he had a love for people that I just didn't have."

The doctor looked away, gazed out the window, saw a distant gentle gathering behind a cloud. The gathering changed gradually to a triple-barred rainbow that held out its shining hand toward the house.

He turned back to Ruth and pointed out the window, encouraging her to look. A little involuntary smile was beginning to gather at the corners of her attractive lips.

As the days went by, the doctor and his young patient got in the habit of sitting on the porch and talking. Dr. Weber poured out all the treasures of his mind and all his powers of tenderness and encouragement upon her.

Ruth's throat was still very tender. One afternoon, as they sat together on the porch, she turned to him and whispered, "I love the musical quality of your voice, Dr. Weber. Would you sing for me?" Angled shade lay sharp as a knife across the warm front yard.

He hesitated. But, he knew he could not refuse.

He hummed a little melody, warming up, then went on to a gala carnival tune.

For a moment, he glanced at her. Clad in a lovely calico dress, the girl was listening intently with a smile of enjoyment.

He sang old German love songs he had heard his parents sing. He sang his heart out while she listened, her eyes never leaving his face. Puffy clouds grazed like wooly sheep across the sky.

Ruth and her doctor decided to take a walk around the large yard. She asked if it would be all right if she let her hair down. Dr. Weber nodded. As she did so, Ruth asked him to keep singing.

She seemed taller tonight than when the doctor had first seen her. Ruth was growing up.

He sang old ballads, river songs he had heard in Portland, hymns. His voice captured things in that yard, things that never change, that never can be changed.

They watched the sun sink slowly beyond the line of the horizon. Slivers of brilliant red streaked the western sky. Across Ruth's shoulders were large, loose curls, brown in shadow, nearly red where the sun's rays touched them.

Lavender and amber hues shot across the thickening purple of oncoming night. Man and girl stood side by side, enthralled, watching God's robe.

Bright points of light appeared before the nearly indigo firmament was clothed. Pale, at first, and coy, they disappeared when initially looked at.

Doctor and patient watched the worlds come twinkling into view, first one by one, then the myriads that no one can count. Soon the stars dwarfed the darkness, lovely as diamonds, soft as forgiveness.

One day Ruth was pronounced well. Dr. Weber said goodbye to the Schafer family and began jogging toward the town where he had left his car. He was looking forward to seeing Ida and the girls. He rested at the top of a hill, then felt the clean cool joy of running down its long slope with the wind in his thinning hair.

He walked along the country road, kicking the dirt, one hand in his pocket, the other holding his bag. Fields of wheat and other crops were everywhere.

A threshing machine was established in front of a nearby farmhouse. Dr. Weber wiped the sweat from his forehead with the sleeve of his jacket and stood watching.

Thirteen men were employed, two throwing down the sheaves of grain from a garner above, two passing them up to the machine, two placing them in the machine, two receiving the straw from the machine, two binding the straw in sheaves, two carrying it away, and the engineman. There was something bloodless about the workers. Each one was all business.

What struck Dr. Weber was the abrupt finish to the process of agriculture. The harvest itself was quite imposing. Then it was thrown to this ruthless machine and, in a moment, amid a puffing and whir of wheels, grains of wheat began to trickle out of the side of it into a sack. Before the day was done, a few sacks leaning against a tree represented all that was really valuable as a result of the year.

The doctor remembered that as he as leaving the Schafer home, Janet had handed him a note, saying, "Ruth wants me to give this to you."

He pulled the sealed envelope from his hip pocket, opened it and began reading the delicate, feminine handwriting:

Dear Dr. Weber,

There are many beautiful things in this world, but I have never known anyone so beautiful as you. Think of what it is to me to have my life back, to have my voice back, to have my throat working properly again, to again feel that I can become a nurse.

I don't think you know this, but I have bent my head over while you were asleep. Many times I have leaned my head down over you, as the sky leaned upon us that night. I have let fall the curls of my hair to cover your precious head. I have folded my hair about you, as the heavens enfolded us. I have wrapped you and wound you during many a long night that I might never lose you.

Ruth

The words were extremely touching, especially considering they were written by such a young girl. The doctor smiled faintly. It seemed strange to him the way a young person sometimes idolized an older one when, really, there was no reason to do so. He had only done his job.

He folded the paper carefully and put it back in his pocket.

CHAPTER SIX

Christmas Eve 1927

The car's heater was on full blast but the cold was winning. Snow-laden pine boughs hung down like giant claws.

People hurried along the road, clutching colorful packages. As the thirty-nine-year-old physician pulled up in front of the stables and stepped from his Chandler sedan, the hairs in his nostrils webbed into instant ice.

Muggs Bentley, a tall teenage boy with a sandy shock of hair combed across his forehead, had just returned to Whitebird, Idaho, after visiting his sweetheart in the State of Washington. It was Saturday, Christmas Eve 1927.

Muggs' burly, good-natured father, Ernest, saw the doctor approaching and said, "Son, I need to have you take Dr. Weber out to the Qualey ranch to see Mrs. Qualey." Marie Qualey had been coughing up blood

51

and was terribly sick. The Qualeys were immigrants from Norway who struggled to make a living fashioning riding equipment such as saddles, bridles and spurs.

"Well, Dr. Weber," said Ernest, reaching up to adjust his cowboy hat, "it's good to see you. Ya know, this is one of the coldest spells I've seen in this country, and I've been here a long time."

"Yeah, Ernest, it certainly is brisk," agreed Dr. Weber, shivering as he chuckled.

The doctor, who lived fifteen miles up the road at Grangeville, pulled his wallet from his hind pocket and paid Ernest for the use of the horses. Wearing an old overcoat and mittens, Dr. Weber swung onto a buckskin mare called Goldie while Muggs mounted King, a big bay horse. It was a little before three in the afternoon.

"But I wanna see Santa Claus!" wailed an insistent boy of about five years old to his mother as they walked along the street, bundled against the cold. Dr. Weber couldn't help but think of the tiny son he had lost a few years earlier while living in Wyoming.

A thermometer attached to a fencepost showed nine degrees below zero as the men headed out in the afternoon mist for Salmon River Canyon. The snow was at least three feet deep.

They rode across the bridge which spanned the Salmon River. Icicles hung from all segments of the structure, adding to and even multiplying its intricate patterns.

The men began the steep climb up the canyon wall, listening to the heavy crunch of the horses' hoofs in the frozen snow. As they followed the mountain trail around abrupt corners, the cold bite of the wind penetrated to their bones.

The path directly ahead seemed to reach into the cloudy sky. The steeds skillfully weaved through the many twists and turns, steaming for the hard work, while swishing willows cut into the men's faces. On they rode, though, toward the ridges that crested the mighty canyon.

At the summit, they stopped to give their horses, and themselves, a breather. The magnificent canyon and the Salmon River lay shrouded in fog below. But they had just begun. It was twenty-five miles to the Qualey ranch on the breaks of the Snake River.

They galloped for about two hours over rolling hills, shuddering with cold. Whirligigs of mountain fog coiled around them like surreal serpents. Muggs turned to the doctor at one point and quipped, "It'll be tough spotting Santa tonight, Dr. Weber."

Rocks and boulders poked their black heads out of the snow while others lay hidden under the drifts and ice, pointed and sharp. The horses were bathed in sweat that crystallized almost immediately, but on they sprinted, their snaky heads stretched forth.

A mist billowed up from the fields of Doumecq Plains. It was one of those fogs that turn everything into an oddly shaped phantom, that muffle and wrap ordinary sounds until they glide to the ear with eerie portent.

Presently, two red-clothed hunters strode through the brush and disappeared into a murky swamp, looking like a couple of Catholic cardinals oozing into a spooky medieval hollow.

A swollen russet moon pushed slowly up through the trees, splayed and scattered among the barren branches by the weird fog. The two men started down a steep hillside, the horses slipping and sliding in thigh-high snow. The riders maneuvered their way along, knowing this was only the first of several rugged ravines between them and the Snake.

The climb up the side of the canyon was very trying, the bite of the wind growing harsher with every step. At times, the route was extremely abrupt and slippery, forcing the horses to climb in a series of leaps so violent the men had to cling to their necks to stay in the saddle. Bands of heavy timber and brush pummeled both horses and riders and caused laden boughs to discharge their burdens on the men's shoulders.

They arrived at the Qualey ranch about midnight. All about them were the dazzling walls of Snake River Canyon, their awesome crests jutting up through the faint moonlight into the firmament. Fog lay over the river, but there was a narrow space between it and the ice. The fog was like a living thing, moving in ways that seemed purposeful. It advanced, then withdrew and advanced again, undulating like an organism.

Rubbing the icicles from his nose, Dr. Weber climbed down from the saddle. He grimaced when he saw that young Muggs' face was covered with a heavy coating of frost, and that his frozen ears were swollen.

The men walked toward the modest house, rubbing sore muscles, Muggs' spurs jingling to announce their arrival. Fog curled up from the branches of an old oak tree like departing souls. Indeed, it would be tough spotting Santa tonight.

The men's faint shadows fell across the porch and lengthened up the heavy log door into the darkness under the eaves. The dark shape of the door suddenly swung outward, and fishtails of light, at top and bottom, shone into the night.

Olaf Qualey wore his brimmed hat at the prescribed country tilt. His thin mouth was so straight it might have been an incision underneath his large nose.

The doctor sat and drummed his frozen fingers against a table for a while in order to get them to bend. Candles had been placed on the branches of a small Christmas tree in clipholders. Stockings had been hung by the chimney with care.

In the bedroom, a large Christmas tree trimmed with candles, tinsel and a few wooden ornaments stood several feet from the fireplace. Mrs. Marie Qualey looked up expectantly as Dr. Weber walked in. Off to the side was a large, table-filled room where the family assembled equipment for horseback riding.

For a while, Marie and the doctor spoke of little things. She was a handsome woman with a look of deep wisdom, someone who had lived much, seen much. She complained of coughing up blood and not being able to sleep at night because of her horrible nightmares of impending death. Still, behind her troubled expression lay the hint of someone who had known joy, hope—even fun. Her middle-aged hair was still the color of winter wheat. It seemed to the doctor that in her eye bobbed the innocent gleam of the little girl next door who still believes in Santa Claus.

He pulled the stethoscope from his bag, listened carefully to her heart and lungs. Then he leaned back in his chair and looked over at the fire, thinking. His spectacles reflected light from candles and tinsel on the Christmas tree. Nevertheless, Marie could see an unspoken sympathy in his face.

Suddenly, one of the young boys, about six years old and cute as a bug's ear, opened the door. He saw Dr. Weber lean close to his mother and say, "I know there's another life, Marie." His voice was as gentle as the lisp of snow against a windowpane.

The boy scampered over and sat down on the bed beside his dear mother. Marie began to feel a little better and got to reminiscing. "I love my children so much," she said with a thick Norwegian accent, hugging the child. "We lost a little boy three years ago. Oh, children, they're so sweet! It's terrible to lose one, Dr. Weber, you just don't know."

She looked at him, noticed the elbows of his shirt were almost out, his knees nearly through his pants. In his blue eyes dwelt an indefinable sadness she hadn't perceived before.

*   *   *

Christmas brownies danced in a long line across the oil cloth tablespread. Steam whistled from a teakettle as the delicious smells of cooking began to fill the air, compliments of two smiling teenage daughters.

Dr. Weber sat at the table, trying to hide the depression he felt, knowing this was the last Christmas the Qualeys would spend together. He would have to tell them the truth.

He got up, motioned Olaf aside and admitted there was nothing he could do for Marie. The tuberculosis would soon kill her. There was a little hospital for such patients about thirty miles to the north, but Mrs. Qualey would have to be hauled out on a stretcher, and he did not believe she could survive the ordeal. All he could do was leave a bottle of pills that offered a little symptomatic relief.

Olaf Qualey buried his withered face in his arms for a few minutes and sobbed bitterly. But eventually he recovered his composure, and the two men returned to their places at the table.

As the Qualeys, Muggs and Dr. Weber ate, Olaf forced a slight smile and asked if each of his children would tell the visitors a little about Christmas in Norway.

A slender boy of twelve or thirteen said that people there adhered strictly to the tradition that passersby, regardless of age or social station, must stop in at every house along the way and partake of food and drink.

Meanwhile, in the next room, Marie Qualey, who had been fed first and then returned to bed, rested comfortably because a wonderful man had come to see her. She hadn't felt this well in a long time.

Ingrid, one of the beautiful teenage Qualey daughters, was dressed in a colorful folk dress from her native land. She told of how, after supper on Christmas Eve, the closed doors which had been hiding the main Christmas tree from the children were suddenly thrown open, with the glittering tree revealed in all its breathless splendor. It was said that, as the Christmas tree filled the room with light, so the star of old shone forth and made the whole world light. The top of the Norwegian Christmas tree was decorated by placing three candles, representing the Three Wise Men, on it. It was believed that the rays of candlelight from the tree bestowed a blessing on whatsoever they gleamed. With this notion in mind, clothes, food and other objects were placed so that the candles would cast their rays on them. And, before retiring on

Christmas Eve, the shoes of all the household were placed in a row as a symbol that the entire family would live peacefully together during the coming year.

Dr. Weber noticed that, in all that was said by the members of the Qualey family, there was no mention of their very trying portage to America, nothing about the difficult journey from the East Coast to Idaho, not a word about their wearisome struggle to survive here on the cold banks of the Snake River. These folks were typical American pioneers: long on hope and hard work, very short on excuses or self-pity.

When the meal was finished and all the Christmas stories had been told, Dr. Weber looked at his young pal, Muggs, and asked, "Are you ready to head back?"

"I'm ready if you are," Muggs replied, surprised that the doctor didn't want to rest for awhile. After all, it was two-thirty in the morning.

"Well, I'm ready to go," said Dr. Weber.

As they were pulling on their coats to leave, Olaf Qualey solemnly pressed a dollar bill into Dr. Weber's hand. The paper was well-worn.

They walked out to the barn. It was so cold the bits had to be warmed over a fire before they were put in the horses' mouths.

While waiting for the bits to warm up, Dr. Weber felt a lump come into his throat, for he knew that all the Qualey shoes would be placed in a row before they retired for the night, and that the bottle of pills would be allowed to catch the magical rays of the three candles at the top of the tree before any would be administered to Marie.

The doctor pulled a clean towel out of his medical bag and insisted that Muggs tie it around his bare ears. The youngster complied. The two men then mounted their horses and started out for the rocky, snowy canyons as heavy fog reached out to embrace them. To the Qualey family, gathered arm in arm at the front window, they were soon diminutive figures in a vast white landscape.

Foam froze to the horses' bridles as they trotted over the rugged terrain. The men felt the sting of pine on cheek and neck while the wind drove splinters of cold through their chests.

The so-called passes were nearly impassable because of deep snow. The horses broke through the crust at times, rearing back to the surface with a tremendous jolt, their legs squirting warm blood into the snow. Coyote voices undulated through the seemingly haunted trees as each brute strained to harmonize with the other.

As the men rode along, the doctor cursed the weather, the snow, the hills, the valleys, his horse, Muggs, the world. He was outdoing even the muleskinners Muggs had worked with.

But the steeds stood up like iron under the terrible work of the journey. Gallantly, they galloped on, regardless of broken ground, deep snow, thick vapors, and spiked rocks that stabbed at them from every side.

Dr. Weber got off his horse at one point to rub his sore knees.

"Doctor, look out behind you!" yelled Muggs.

Dr. Weber glanced back and saw a hungry-eyed coyote slithering toward him. Quickly, his knees weren't so painful and he leaped back into the saddle.

It was eleven in the morning when they rode across the Salmon River Bridge just outside Whitebird, creatures of ice, at one with the winter. Fog hung mournfully from the trees on the bank. The doctor's lips had cracked as crisply as a piece of hard toast, and then frozen. His eyes were swollen almost shut. The bellies and legs of the horses were caked thick and hard with the butchery of many a stabbing stone.

At the side of the road sat a humble little cottage. On the chimney hung a sign written in a child's handwriting, "SANTA, PLEASE STOP HERE."

"Do you suppose there really is a Santa Claus, Dr. Weber?" asked Muggs.

The doctor's response totally surprised the young horseman. "Oh, you know the the old saying, Muggs. 'Yes, Virginia, there really is a Santa Claus. Just as surely as love and generosity and devotion exist, he exists. What a dreary world it would be without Santa!'" Even though his face was disfigured, Dr. Weber had a wonderful smile as he spoke. He seemed to glow.

From a church came the muffled sound of an organ as the men rode into town. Ironically, a choir burst into "God Rest Ye Merry Gentlemen."

An old mule was frozen in a crouching position just to the left of the stables. Dr. Weber soon found his car was frozen too. Muggs located some wood alcohol in a shed, and together they succeeded in getting the vehicle started.

As he was about to drive off, Dr. Weber pressed the worn dollar bill into Muggs' hand. "Merry Christmas, Muggs," he said. Then the car rolled away into the patches of fog and headed up the precarious ice of

Whitebird Hill toward Grangeville. It was something like trying to drive up a narrow ice skating lane with a steep canyon on the right side.

Muggs shuffled into the house and fell across his bed, sleeping until evening. His mother, Julia Bentley, went into the bedroom and coaxed him into joining the family in what remained of Christmas dinner.

"Well, how did the trip go last night, son?" asked Ernest.

Munching a turkey leg, Muggs said, "Well, it was a cold, tough ride, but we made it."

"Is Mrs. Qualey going to be all right?" asked Julia.

"Oh, no," replied Muggs. "Dr. Weber says she has tuberculosis and it's far advanced. She won't live long."

"The thing I can't understand," said Ernest, shaking his head, "is why Dr. Weber went out there at all. He must have known that with Mrs. Qualey coughing up blood the way she was, there was nothing he could do. And everybody knows those people don't have any money. Why on earth would he go to all that trouble just to see a hopeless case?"

"Yeah, I wondered about that too, Dad."

Muggs finished chewing on the drumstick and set it on his plate. His younger brothers and sisters were talking animatedly about the gifts they had received for Christmas. Still not feeling well, Muggs excused himself from the table and went into his bedroom.

He stepped to the window and gazed out. The fog had lifted and the moonlight was radiant. A lovely deer poked its head out of the woods, surveying the scene. Muggs watched the animal scout around for food for a while, then head up a slight incline.

Stretching out on the bed, Muggs thought of his sweetheart, Jettie Lyda. They would marry as soon as she finished high school.

Jettie was the perfect girl for him, that he knew. She had grown up on a ranch on Doumecq Plains until going recently to Asotin, Washington, to attend school. She loved living in the country as much as he did. They'd have a ranch, no doubt, and several children.

He thought of the winter that Jettie lay ill at her parents' home on Doumecq Plains, and of how worried he had been that she wouldn't make it. Dr. Weber had made several very difficult trips to their place and pulled her through the illness.

But the bitter ride he and the doctor had made the night before was altogether different. He shivered at the thought. Why had they gone out there, freezing their tails off, risking their necks the way they did? Mrs. Qualey was simply too old and sick to recover.

Muggs yawned. He dozed. When he awoke, he wasn't sure how much time had elapsed. The house was quiet. Apparently, everyone had gone to bed.

Feeling a little better, he climbed out of bed and opened the door. There was a light in the study.

His large bare feet pattered their way across the kitchen floor. Shyly, he leaned in the doorway to see who was there.

"Oh, hi, Muggs," said his father, putting aside the book he was reading. "What can I help you with?"

"Oh, I'm all right, Dad. Still a little weak is all."

"Sure. Say, why don't you help yourself to some of that turkey in the fridge?"

"Believe I will." Muggs stared sheepishly at his feet, wondering if what he wanted to say was foolish. "Dad, I've been thinking. Seems to me Dr. Weber just wanted to say, 'Mrs. Qualey, somebody cares.'"

Marie Qualey died three weeks after the two men's trip to see her.

ABOUT THE AUTHOR

Tom Weber was born at Boise, Idaho, in 1946. He received a bachelors degree in Political Science from Brigham Young University in 1970 and a Juris Doctor degree from the University of Utah in 1973. Through the years he has worked for a number of governmental agencies, including the Utah State Insurance Fund and the United States Tariff Commission.

While growing up in southern Idaho, Mr. Weber accompanied his father on many of his house calls. He resides at Salt Lake City.

"As I began to earnestly research his life," recalls the author, "and caught a glimpse of his enormous achievement, I sensed my unworthiness to search further. I was treading on holy ground. It was like entering a sacred shrine and involuntarily dropping to one's knees in awe. Still, I determined to stay the course despite my weakness since no one else was likely to ever do so."

The author can be reached at tomweber7@yahoo. com or at P.O. Box 1321, West Jordan, UT 84084.

CPSIA information can be obtained at www.ICGtesting.com
Printed in the USA
BVOW03s2143100314

347257BV00002B/116/P

9 781491 815618